TENERIFE

HIKING GUIDE

2024

Your guide to Natural Splendor, Cultural Richness, and Adventurous spirit in Spain Island.

Christopher Levell

Tenerife hiking guide

Copyright

Christopher Levell © 2023. All rights reserved

Before this document is duplicated or reproduced in any manner, the publisher's consent must be gained.

Therefore, the contents within can neither be stored electronically, transferred, nor kept in a database. Neither in part nor in full can the document be copied, scanned, faxed, or retained without approval from the publisher or creator.

TABLE OF CONTENTS

1. **INTRODUCTION TO TENERIFE HIKING**
   Overview of Tenerife
   Reasons to Hike in Tenerife
   Types of Hikes in Tenerife
   Planning Your Tenerife Hiking Trip
2. **HIKING REGIONS OF TENERIFE**
   1. Exploring the Teide National Park
   2. Exploring the Anaga Mountains
   3. Enchanting Teno Mountains of Tenerife
   4. The Enchanting Orotava Valley of Tenerife
   5. The Enchanting South Coast of Tenerife
3. **DETAILED HIKING TRAILS**
4. **HIKING ESSENTIALS**
   1. What to pack for a Tenerife hike
   2. A Guide to Getting Around Tenerife:
   3. Leaving No Trace Principles :
   4. Hiking Etiquette:
5. **ADDITIONAL INFORMATION**
   1. Best time to hike in Tenerife
   2. Getting to and around Tenerife:
   3. Accommodations in Tenerife
   4. Food and drink in Tenerife

CONCLUSION

1. INTRODUCTION TO TENERIFE HIKING

Overview of Tenerife

Tenerife, the biggest and most populated island of the Canary Islands, is a volcanic paradise boasting a diversified scenery that runs from lush forests and majestic mountains to parched deserts and volcanic plains. With its gorgeous landscape, agreeable temperature, and well-maintained routes, Tenerife is a hiker's ideal vacation.

Reasons to Hike in Tenerife

- **Unique Landscape**: Tenerife's volcanic origins have produced a landscape of exceptional beauty, with towering peaks, deep ravines, and bizarre rock formations. Hiking helps you to immerse yourself in these wonderful surroundings.
- **Variety of Trails**: Tenerife provides a wide network of hiking routes, catering to all levels of expertise, from leisurely strolls through beautiful valleys to demanding ascents to the top of Mount Teide, Spain's highest mountain.

- **Pleasant Climate**: Tenerife offers a pleasant environment year-round, with high temperatures and low rainfall, making it a perfect area to trek throughout the year.

- **Rich Biodiversity**: Tenerife's various habitats, from laurel woods to lava plains, sustain a broad range of plant and animal species. Hiking offers a chance to see this unique biodiversity.

- **Cultural Heritage**: Tenerife's hiking paths typically pass through traditional communities and historical places, allowing a look into the island's rich cultural past.

Types of Hikes in Tenerife

- **Easy Hikes:** These routes are appropriate for novices and families, with gradual inclines and well-maintained pathways.

- **Moderate Hikes**: These paths involve greater physical effort, with steeper inclines and longer lengths.

- **Challenging Hikes**: These paths are for experienced hikers, featuring steep ascents, difficult terrain, and high elevations.

Planning Your Tenerife Hiking Trip

1. Choose the Right Time: The ideal season to trek in Tenerife is during the spring (March-May) or autumn (September-November) when the weather is moderate and there is less rainfall.

2. Select the Right Trails: Choose trails that match your fitness level and experience. Read route descriptions and examine maps to understand the terrain and difficulties.

3. Pack Properly: Pack suitable clothes, footwear, and gear for the weather and terrain conditions. Bring lots of water, snacks, and sunscreen.

4. Check Weather Forecasts: Be careful of weather conditions and plan your treks appropriately. Avoid trekking in harsh conditions such as heavy rain or high gusts.

5. Inform Others: Let someone know where you are going and when you anticipate to return.

6. Respect the Environment: Leave no evidence of your presence and respect the natural environment.

2. HIKING REGIONS OF TENERIFE

1. Exploring the Teide National Park

Introduction

The Teide National Park, a UNESCO World Heritage Site, is a volcanic paradise situated on the island of Tenerife in the Canary Islands. It is home to Mount Teide, Spain's highest peak, and has a spectacular scenery of lava flows, rock formations, and distinctive flora and wildlife. With its broad assortment of hiking paths, the park provides an amazing journey for nature aficionados and outdoor adventurers.

Hiking Trails in Teide National Park

Embark on a moderate journey in the center of Teide National Park, starting at the Chinyero Visitor Center and ascending towards the Roques de García, famous rock formations resembling a petrified castle. Enjoy magnificent views at the peak of Mount Teide and the surrounding volcanic landscape.

Mount Teide via Montaña Blanca

Challenge yourself with this hard climb that goes to the top of Mount Teide, Spain's highest mountain. Ascend through the Teide Field of Pumice, a sea of volcanic rock, and reach the famed Altavista Mountain Refuge, giving breathtaking views of the crater and the surrounding islands.

Tamaimo Circular Route

Explore the Tamaimo Circular Route, an easy walk that travels through the Tamaimo Ravine, giving varied flora and spectacular views of the Roques de García and Mount Teide. Discover the unique flora and animals of the area, including wild Canary Island cabbage palms.

Chinyero and Narices del Teide

Witness the force of nature on this easy climb that goes to the Chinyero Volcano, the youngest volcano on Tenerife. Explore the lava flows and volcanic cones, and view the Narices del Teide, rock formations resembling huge noses.

Roques de García Forest

Immerse yourself in the Roques de García Forest, a unique geological marvel distinguished by odd rock formations, twisted pines, and a serene ambiance.

Discover the unique biodiversity of the forest, including rare flora and wildlife.

The Forest of the Enchanted Laurels: This simple walk leads you into the heart of the laurel forest, passing past waterfalls and old trees.

Afur-Cruz de Carmen: This moderate walk weaves its way up the slope, affording beautiful views of the Anaga coast and the Roques de Anaga rock formations.

Cruz del Carmen-Punta del Hidalgo: This tough path follows the edge of the Anaga Mountains, affording panoramic views of the shoreline and the nearby islands.

2. Exploring the Anaga Mountains

The Anaga Mountains are home to a network of ravines, deep canyons created by old volcanic rivers. These ravines are a home for unusual flora and animals, and they provide breathtaking beauty. Some of the more popular ravines are the Barranco del Infierno and the Barranco de Afur.

Scattered across the Anaga Mountains are lovely towns that cling to the hills, providing a peek of the island's traditional way of life. Visit the town of Chamorga, noted for its traditional architecture and local crafts, or stop by the village of Taganana, a charming fishing community with spectacular views of the coastline.

Unveiling the Secrets of the Coast

The Anaga coast is a rough and scenic piece of coastline, with stunning cliffs, quiet bays, and secret beaches. Take a boat excursion around the shore to explore the hidden beauties of the Anaga coast, or trek along the coastal pathways to enjoy the spectacular views.

Preserving the Anaga Mountains

The Anaga Mountains are a delicate ecology, and it is crucial to preserve and maintain this natural gem. When visiting the Anaga Mountains, adopt the Leave No Trace guidelines to minimize your influence on the ecosystem. Stick to authorized pathways, prevent trash, and respect the flora and animals.

The Anaga Mountains are a remarkable treasure of Tenerife, presenting a unique combination of natural beauty, cultural legacy, and ecological value. Whether you are a seasoned hiker or a nature enthusiast, the Anaga Mountains will leave you breathless with their beautiful landscape, rich biodiversity, and quiet environment. Come and explore the mysteries of the Anaga Mountains and enjoy the charm of Tenerife.

3. Enchanting Teno Mountains of Tenerife

Introduction

Rising majestically from the northern edge of Tenerife, the Teno Mountains serve as a tribute to the island's volcanic origins and breathtaking natural beauty. This craggy mountain, a dramatic contrast to the sun-kissed beaches and bush resorts of Tenerife's south, provides a retreat for hikers, nature enthusiasts, and those seeking a peek into the island's real personality.

A Landscape of Volcanic Wonders

The Teno Mountains: are a geological paradise, created by millions of years of volcanic activity. Deep ravines, produced by ancient rivers cutting their way through the volcanic environment, separate the mountains into various regions, each with its own particular character. The Masca Gorge, a stunning gorge tumbling towards the shore, is a must-visit for brave hikers.

Monte del Agua: A green woodland situated within the volcanic environment, gives a nice relief from the sun-exposed pathways. The forest is home to a vast range of plant life, including old laurel woods and rare species found nowhere else on Earth.

Punta de Teno: The westernmost point of Tenerife, is a photographer's paradise. Dramatic cliffs falling into the Atlantic Ocean, the horizon reaching forever towards the horizon, and the ever-changing play of light and shadow create spectacular vistas.

Exploring the Hidden Trails

The Teno Mountains provide a network of routes catering to all kinds of hikers, from pleasant strolls along the shore to demanding ascents into the mountains' center. Here are a handful of the more popular trails:

Los Cristianos to Teno Alto: This gentle walk weaves its way up the mountainsides, affording spectacular views of the beach and the neighboring communities.

Erjos: This simple walk takes you through the town of Erjos, a typical settlement with whitewashed cottages and small alleyways, and then on to a magnificent vantage point.

Santiago del Teide to Masca: This tough trek traverses the Masca Gorge, affording amazing views of the valley and the surrounding mountains.

Discovering the Cultural Heritage

The Teno Mountains are home to lovely settlements that have kept the island's traditional way of life. Visit the town of Masca, hidden in the Masca Gorge, and meander through its small alleys and whitewashed cottages. Stop by the town of Santiago del Teide, a charming community with a rich history and spectacular views of the Teide National Park.

A Sanctuary for Wildlife

The Teno Mountains provide a shelter for a variety of animals, including the endangered Barbary falcon, the Tenerife gigantic lizard, and the Canary Islands buzzard. Keep your eyes alert while you trek, and you may be fortunate enough to see one of these fascinating species.

Preserving the Teno Mountains

The Teno Mountains are a delicate ecology, and it is crucial to preserve and maintain this natural gem. When visiting the Teno Mountains, practice the Leave No Trace guidelines to limit your influence on the ecosystem. Stick to authorized pathways, prevent trash, and respect the flora and animals.

The Teno Mountains are a hidden jewel of Tenerife, presenting a combination of natural beauty, cultural legacy, and ecological value. Whether you are an expert hiker or a nature enthusiast, the Teno Mountains will leave you breathless with their beautiful landscape, rich biodiversity, and quiet environment. Come and explore the mysteries of the Teno Mountains and feel the beauty of Tenerife.

4. The Enchanting Orotava Valley of Tenerife

Introduction

Nestled between the breathtaking slopes of Mount Teide, the Orotava Valley is a patchwork of green landscapes, fascinating communities, and enthralling history. This lush valley, running from the north shore to the slopes of Mount Teide, has been the core of Tenerife's culture and agriculture for generations.

A Valley of Contrasts

The Orotava Valley is a world of opposites, where volcanic vistas meet lush foliage, lively cities combine with calm villages, and contemporary life coexists with rich traditions. The valley's lush soil has fostered a vibrant agricultural business, providing an abundance of bananas, grapes, and other crops.

Mount Teide, Spain's tallest mountain, sits as a sentinel above the Orotava Valley, its towering presence molding the valley's scenery and culture. The volcano's distinctive geology and diversified ecosystems have earned it UNESCO World Heritage Site designation.

A Haven for Hikers and Nature Enthusiasts

The Orotava Valley provides a paradise for hikers and environment lovers, with a network of routes catering to all levels of expertise. From relaxing strolls through banana fields to strenuous ascents into the mountains, the valley affords a range of possibilities to appreciate its natural splendor.

The valley is home to various botanical gardens, such as the La Orotava Botanical Garden and the Jardín Botánico de Puerto de la Cruz, which display the island's rich biodiversity and give a calm respite among the valley's lively communities.

A Journey through History and Culture

The Orotava Valley is rich in history, with its towns and villages enjoying a legacy of traditional architecture and cultural heritage. La Orotava, the valley's biggest town, is a treasure trove of antique structures, notably the Casa del Balcón, with its characteristic wooden balconies.

La Laguna, a UNESCO World Heritage Site, is another treasure of the Orotava Valley. Its old core, with its cobblestone walkways, colonial buildings, and colorful plazas, gives a look into Tenerife's rich history.

Unveiling the Secrets of Wine and Gastronomy

The Orotava Valley is known for its wine making legacy, with vineyards producing some of Tenerife's most acclaimed wines. Visit one of the valley's wineries to learn about the region's distinct winemaking processes and experience the flavors of the valley's terroir.

The valley's gastronomic scene is a symphony of flavors, with traditional Canarian food taking center stage. Indulge in native dishes like papas (wrinkled potatoes), mojo picón (spicy sauce), and gofio (roasted cornmeal).

A Living Legacy of Traditions

The Orotava Valley comes alive during its bright festivals, such as the Fiesta del Corpus Christi, a UNESCO Intangible Cultural Heritage of Humanity, which features exquisite floral carpets and religious processions.

The valley is also a hub for traditional handicrafts, with craftsmen making ceramics, textiles, and other handcrafted goods that represent the island's past.

Preserving the Orotava Valley

The Orotava Valley is a delicate combination of human activity and natural beauty. It is crucial to respect and conserve the valley's ecosystem and legacy while visiting. Follow the Leave No Trace principles, support local businesses, and enjoy the unique beauty of this beautiful valley.

The Orotava Valley is a compelling combination of natural beauties, cultural legacy, and active customs. Whether you are a history lover, a nature enthusiast, or a seeker of real experiences, the Orotava Valley will leave you fascinated with its timeless beauty and kind welcome.

5. The Enchanting South Coast of Tenerife

Introduction

The South Coast of Tenerife, a sun-kissed paradise, is a draw for travelers seeking leisure, adventure, and cultural immersion. This bustling area, ranging from Los Cristianos to Adeje, has a stunning combination of beautiful beaches, quaint villages, and adrenaline activities.

A Haven of Beaches and Watersports

The South Coast is famed for its gorgeous beaches, providing a refuge for sunbathers, swimmers, and water sports lovers. Playa de Las Américas, with its vibrant environment, is a popular option for families and friends. For a more quiet experience, travel to Playa del Duque, noted for its opulent facilities and clean seas.

El Médano Beach, a windsurfing paradise, draws adrenaline seekers from across the world. The steady winds and waves make it a fantastic site for riding the waves, while the tranquil waters of Las Gaviotas Beach offer a wonderful hideaway for snorkeling and kayaking.

A Journey through Thriving Towns and Villages

The South Coast is home to a variety of towns and villages, each giving its distinct beauty and character. Los Cristianos, the region's busy tourist center, provides a dynamic nightlife, an abundance of shops and restaurants, and a cosmopolitan ambiance.

Playa de los Cristianos, a lovely seaside village, offers a calm and welcoming environment. Stroll along the promenade, eat a delicious seafood lunch, or shop through the local markets.

Adeje, a wealthy resort town, is noted for its expensive hotels, world-class golf courses, and attractive retail complexes. Explore the town's quaint pedestrian walkways, engage in relaxing spa treatments, or relish exquisite food at Michelin-starred restaurants.

Adventures & Excursions

The South Coast is a playground for adventure lovers, providing a varied selection of activities and excursions. Take a thrilling trip on the Siam Park water slides, discover the undersea world with a scuba diving or snorkeling excursion, or go on a breathtaking climb to the top of Mount Teide, Spain's highest mountain.

Embark on a whale-watching expedition to view the spectacular marine life that inhabits the seas off

Tenerife's shore. Dolphins, pilot whales, and even sperm whales may be sighted with a little luck.

Visit Loro Parque, a famous wildlife conservation park, to experience parrots, penguins, and other exotic species. Immerse yourself in the park's spectacular entertainment and instructive exhibitions.

Preserving the South Coast's Beauty

The South Coast's natural beauty and dynamic ecosystems are priceless gems. When visiting the area, employ sustainable tourist practices to limit your influence on the ecosystem. Choose eco-friendly hotels, save water, and dispose of garbage ethically.

A Destination for All

The South Coast of Tenerife caters to a varied spectrum of guests, from families seeking coastal fun to couples seeking romantic holidays and adventure enthusiasts seeking adrenaline-pumping activities. With its combination of natural beauty, cultural attractions, and contemporary comforts, the South Coast provides a wonderful experience for everybody.

Come and explore the magnificent South Coast of Tenerife, where leisure, adventure, and cultural immersion await.

3. DETAILED HIKING TRAILS

1. Teide: from Chinyero to the Roques de García

Amidst Tenerife's volcanic terrain, the spectacular Mount Teide, Spain's highest mountain, stands sentinel. Its slopes provide a range of paths, each with their own special rewards and difficulties. Hiking the Teide walk from Chinyero to Roques de García trail is a moderate trek that reveals an amazing world of indigenous plants, rock formations, and lava flows.

Overview of Trail
- Depth: 7.2 miles (4.5 km)
- Time: two to three hours
- Moderate in difficulty
- An increase in elevation: 213 meters (701 feet)

Point of origin:

The Chinyero Visitor Centre, which is situated on the TF-38 highway, is where the route starts. The tourist center has plenty of parking spaces.

Description of Route:
Ascend into the Chinyero volcanic caldera by following the path markers from the tourist center. In 1909, a volcanic explosion created this region.

Tenerife hiking guide

The route offers breathtaking views of the surrounding area as it goes through the lava flows.

You will travel through many little ravines and a pine forest as you continue on the trek. Considering the volcanic terrain, this location has remarkably abundant flora.

Approximately 2.5 km will get you to the Roques de García. The odd designs carved into these rock formations are a product of wind erosion. Spend some time exploring the surroundings and taking in the vistas from the top of the .

The route heads towards the TF-21 motorway after about 2 km from the Roques de García. Ascend to the Mirador de Sámara by crossing the roadway and following the designated route. Views of the surrounding mountains and the Teide caldera are expansive from this vantage point.

The route returns to the Chinyero Visitor Centre after descending from the Mirador de Sámara.

Protective Measures:

- Don't forget to pack lots of water and sunscreen, and wear supportive hiking shoes.
- If it has been raining, use caution as the track might become slick
- Before trekking, make sure you acclimatize yourself since the altitude might be high in certain places.

Further Advice:

- To avoid the heat, start your walk early in the morning if you're going during the summer.
- Refreshments are available in the Chinyero Visitor Center's little café.
- Carry a camera to record the breathtaking vistas as you travel the path.

Teide National Park's volcanic scenery is best experienced on this walk. It is an excellent option for both seasoned and inexperienced hikers because of its moderate difficulty and breathtaking views.

I'm hoping your walk is a huge success!

2. Scaling Mount Teide with Montaña Blanca

Amidst Tenerife's volcanic scenery, the spectacular Mount Teide, Spain's highest peak and a UNESCO World Heritage Site, towers over the landscape. Gaining access to the pinnacle of this magnificent hill, which offers amazing sweeping views of the island and beyond, is an experience that will never be forgotten. Hiking the Montaña Blanca path to Mount Teide is a strenuous but rewarding experience that passes through a variety of environments, from verdant woods to desolate volcanic plains.

Trail Summary
- Length: 7.2 miles (11.6 km)
- Time: five to six hours
- Level of difficulty: Hard
- Gaining 1,194 meters in elevation (3,917 ft)

Beginning Point:

Montaña Blanca, a mountain pass around 25 km from La Orotava, is where the trek starts. The trailhead has a limited amount of parking.

Route Synopsis:

The trail's first ascent through a pine grove provides a pleasant break from the heat. You will leave the woodland and reach a desolate volcanic environment as you ascend higher. This portion of the hike offers just stunning vistas.

You will arrive at the Altavista Mountain Refuge, a well-liked location for hikers to stop and replenish, after traveling around 3 km. Because the refuge is

3,550 meters (11,647 feet) above sea level, you should adjust to the altitude before proceeding.

The route continues going upwards from the Altavista Mountain Refuge in the direction of Mount Teide's peak. The hardest part of the path is the last stretch, which has loose scree and steep inclines. But every step is worthwhile because of the sights at the summit.

You will be rewarded with expansive views over Tenerife, the nearby islands of La Gomera, La Palma, and El Hierro, and on a clear day, even the peak of Mount Atlas in Morocco, after you reach the top of Mount Teide. Spend some time admiring the scenery and relishing your sense of achievement.

The path for the descent and climb is the same. On the loose screen, take your time and use caution.

Safety Measures:
- Make sure you pack lots of water and sunscreen, and wear supportive hiking footwear.

- If it has been raining, use caution as the walk may get slick.
- Make sure you acclimatize yourself before trekking since the altitude might be high in certain places.
- Pace yourself and take breaks when necessary since the latter half of the trek may be rather difficult.
- If you are not in excellent physical shape, you may want to think about going for a shorter or easier walk.
- Because the weather on the mountain may change quickly, be sure to check the weather prediction before you go.

Extra Advice:

- In order to avoid the heat, start your walk early in the morning if it's during the summer.
- Refreshments are available at the Montaña Blanca trailhead at a small café.

- To record the breathtaking vistas along the walk, pack a camera.
- Leave no evidence of your visit and treat the environment with reverence.

You will reach the peak of one of the most famous volcanoes in the world on this strenuous but worthwhile walk. It is an absolute must-do for every hiker visiting Tenerife, because of its stunning vistas and varied landscapes.

3. The Tamaimo Circular Route

Hiking along Tenerife's Tamaimo Circular Route, which winds through charming communities, beautiful valleys, and stunning vistas, is a great way to spend time outdoors. Hikers of all skill levels may enjoy this modest trek, which highlights the island's natural beauty and cultural legacy.

Overview of Trail

- Distance: 5.7 miles (3.5 km)
- Time: Four hours

- Moderate in difficulty
- Altitude Gain: 1,657 feet, or 505 meters

Point of origin:

The picturesque town of Tamaimo, which is part of the municipality of Santiago del Teide, is where the walk starts. There is plenty of parking in the village.

Description of Route:

The route leaves Tamaimo and climbs gradually past terraced hills and cultivated fields, providing sweeping views of the surrounding valley and the imposing Mount Teide. You will come across the ruins of old water canals as you get higher, relics from the island's agricultural past.

The route turns towards the Barranco Manchas de Las Díaz, a striking ravine sculpted by volcanic activity, upon arriving at the Degollada del Roque mountain. With breath-taking vistas of the valley below, the walk travels along the brink of the ravine.

You will see several lava flows and rock formations throughout the route, which are evidence of Tenerife's previous volcanic activity. A number of rare plant species are also visible along the walk, such as the Canary Island cabbage palm, which represents the island's exceptional biodiversity.

A string of Tibetan prayer flags at the trail's highest point will greet you and provide a spiritual element to the surroundings. Pause for a minute to enjoy the expansive views of the surrounding mountains, the coastline, and the Barranco Manchas de Las Díaz.

After that, the route descends in the direction of Arguayo hamlet while winding through a pine forest and volcanic rocks. When you arrive at Arguayo, spend some time admiring the peaceful ambiance and the historic architecture of the hamlet.

The road winds through farms and past the striking "Cross of the Missionaries," a memorial to the island's religious heritage, as it returns to Tamaimo from Arguayo.

There are uneven and steep parts of the descent to Tamaimo, so you'll need to use caution while walking. But the descent is definitely worth it for the vistas of the surrounding countryside and the settlement.

Protective Measures:

- Don't forget to pack lots of water and sunscreen, and wear supportive hiking shoes.
- If it has been raining, use caution as the track might become slick.
- Exercise care on the trail's steeper parts and be aware of the uneven ground.
- Be mindful of the surrounding environment and remove any signs of your visit.

Further Advice:
- To avoid the heat, start your walk early in the morning if you're going during the summer.
- You may have a light lunch or snack at any one of Tamaimo's many cafés and eateries.
- Carry a camera to record the breathtaking vistas as you travel the path.

Hiking along the Tamaimo Circular Route is a lovely way to take in the natural beauty, cultural legacy, and stunning perspectives of the area. It is the ideal option for hikers of all skill levels looking for an amazing journey in Tenerife because of its moderate difficulty and varied sceneries.

4. Exploring the Volcanic Wonders of Narices de Teide and Chinyero

Tenerife is a volcanic island in the Canary Islands that offers a compelling environment of distinctive flora and wildlife, as well as rock formations and lava flows. The Chinyero volcano and the Narices del Teide, two recognisable rock formations that bear witness to the island's volcanic history, are only two of its numerous natural wonders.

Witness to Volcanic Power:

Chinyero Volcano

Tenerife's northwest Chinyero volcano serves as a reminder of the volcanic activity that had occurred there. In 1909, this very young volcano erupted, producing a new cone and a sea-level lava flow. The eruption produced breathtaking ash plumes that rose up to 7 kilometers (4.3 miles) in the air.

A famous tourist site today, the Chinyero volcano gives tourists a look into the island's volcanic past. A diverse range of flora, including ferns and mosses, cover the slopes of the volcano, and the lava flows provide indigenous species a special home.

The "Noses of Teide " are Narices del Teide.

The two rock formations known as the Narices de Teide, or "Noses of Teide" in Spanish, are situated close to the top of Mount Teide, the highest mountain in Spain. These odd-looking structures, which resemble enormous noses, are the product of millennia of wind erosion.

Photographers love the Narices de Teide because of its breathtaking vistas of the surrounding countryside, which includes Mount Teide and the volcanic caldera. With several routes going to their base, the formations are a well-liked hiking attraction as well.

Exploration of Volcanic Terrain

Immersing oneself in the island's volcanic scenery by hiking to the Chinyero volcano and the Narices del Teide is an amazing experience. A moderate walk leads past the volcano's cone and through the lava flows on the Chinyero Trail. The path takes two to three hours to finish and is about 3.5 kilometers (2.2 miles) long.

For a more strenuous walk that ascends to the summit of the rock formations, try the Narices de Teide Trail. The path is around 2.8 miles (4.5 km) long and takes 3–4 hours to finish.

Safety Measures to Take and Extra Advice:

- Make sure you pack lots of water and sunscreen, and wear supportive hiking footwear.
- If it has been raining, use caution as the paths may become slick.
- Make sure you acclimatize yourself before trekking since the altitude might be high in certain places.
- In order to avoid the heat, start your walk early in the morning if it's during the summer.

- Near the trailheads are a number of cafés and restaurants where you may have a little lunch or snack.
- Bring a camera so you may record the breathtaking vistas seen along the paths.

Leave no evidence of your visit and treat the environment with respect.

Trekking up the Narices de Teide and Chinyero volcanoes is a worthwhile adventure that provides a unique viewpoint on the island's volcanic past. You will be astounded by the beauty and importance of these natural marvels with their striking landscapes and alluring rock formations. Come see Tenerife's volcanic beauties and set off on a once-in-a-lifetime journey.

5. Entering the Enchanted Forest of Roques de García

The Roques de García Forest is a beautiful refuge of volcanic rock formations, luscious foliage, and engaging fauna, nestled inside the heart of

Tenerife's Teide National Park. A must-visit location for both nature lovers and adventurers, this enchanted woodland is called for the notable rock spires that rise from its depths. It provides a unique combination of natural beauty and geological marvels.

A Wonder of Geology

The island's volcanic history is shown by the Roques de García Forest. These strange and alluring rock formations, called , are the result of lava flows that hardened millions of years ago. They are like sentinels among the lush forest. Over generations, wind erosion has carved these , some of which reach heights of over 50 meters (164 feet), producing an unearthly environment that resembles a petrified forest.

A Biodiversity Haven

Biodiversity abounds in the Roques de García Forest, despite its volcanic beginnings. With its sheltering valleys and diverse terrain, the forest's distinct microclimate fosters a wide variety of plant and animal life. Amidst the lava-strewn ground, pine trees, Canary Island cabbage palms, and a variety of unique flora and wildflowers flourish.

A wide variety of wildlife may also be discovered in the forest, such as the fascinating Tenerife lizard, which is unique to this part of the globe. The kestrel, buzzard, and Berthelot's pipit—a little bird unique to the Canary Islands—are some of the other noteworthy residents.

A Discovery Path

A network of well-maintained hiking routes crisscrosses the Roques de García Forest, giving tourists plenty of chances to discover its natural treasures. The rather difficult Sendero 3 trek meanders through the forest, providing up-close looks at the and the varied vegetation.

You'll come across relics from the forest's history along the walk, such as historic charcoal furnaces that the island's residents once used years ago. The route also leads to a number of overlooks that provide expansive views of the surrounding terrain, including Spain's highest peak, the spectacular Mount Teide.

A Place of Refuge for the Senses

All of the senses are stimulated during a hiking trip at the Roques de García Forest. The flora and fauna's vivid colors create an enthralling visual panorama, while the cool mountain air fills your lungs with the sound of rustling leaves.

Spend some time enjoying the distinct textures of the volcanic rocks, the subtle scents of the flowers, and the soft swaying of the branches in the air as you stroll through the forest. The serenity and quiet of the forest offers a much-needed break from the daily grind, enabling you to rediscover the natural world and attain inner tranquility.

A Trip Into The Arms of Nature

A site of wonder and enchantment, the Roques de García Forest displays the beauty of nature via a tapestry of volcanic landforms, lush flora, and a variety of fauna. You may go on an exploration voyage there and lose yourself in the tranquility and beauty of Tenerife's natural heritage. So grab your spirit of adventure, lace up your hiking boots, and get ready to be enchanted by the magical Roques de García Forest.

6. Explore the Enchanting Tenerife Laurel Forest

Tucked away in the lush slopes of Anaga, the northeasternmost peak of Tenerife, is the UNESCO World Heritage Site and beautiful natural marvel that is the Laurel Forest. With its rich foliage, varied flora, and enthralling atmosphere, this old forest—a remnant of the Tertiary period—has acquired the nickname "Forest of the Enchanted Laurels."

A Emerald Hue Realm

With a vast canopy of towering laurel trees, or laurisilva, that filters sunlight and creates an ethereal ambiance, the Laurel Forest, which covers more than 37,000 acres, is a captivating tapestry of green colors. These old trees, some of which may grow to heights of over 30 meters (98 feet), have flourished for millions of years in this special habitat, and their survival is evidence of the forest's eternal beauty.

The lush understory of ferns, mosses, and other plant life that thrives under the laurisilva canopy adds to the forest's allure. The forest floor is covered with delicate orchids, vivid wildflowers, and aromatic plants that entice the senses with a symphony of hues and fragrances.

A Biodiversity Haven

Numerous plant and animal species, many of which are unique to Tenerife or the Canary Islands, may be found in abundance in the Laurel Forest. The distinct microclimate of the forest, which is marked by high humidity, comfortable temperatures, and copious amounts of rainfall, makes for the perfect environment for a healthy ecology.

The Canary Islands lizard, a charming reptile well-known for its sun-loving habits, and the plump, colorful Tenerife laurel pigeon are two of the forest's residents. Invertebrates of many kinds, such as spiders, moths, and butterflies, find shelter in the forest and help maintain the complex biological balance of the area.

A Peaceful and Enchanting Realm

Entering the Laurel Forest is like entering another universe—one of peace and magic. The only noises outside are the soft rustle of leaves and the sporadic cry of birds. The air is fresh and chilly.

The pathways in the forest allow visitors to fully immerse themselves in this magical realm as they wander through the thick foliage. Spend some time admiring the complex beauty of the trees, the delicate flowers, and the moss-covered rocks that border the trails as you stroll along them.

A Conservation Legacy

Tenerife's Laurel Forest is an invaluable natural resource, and protecting it is crucial. Because of the fragility of the forest's unique ecology, human-caused dangers including pollution, invading species, and deforestation must be avoided.

The creation of protected areas, the use of sustainable tourism strategies, and the encouragement of environmental education are all part of the ongoing conservation efforts to preserve the Laurel Forest. The goal of these initiatives is to guarantee that future generations will continue to find wonder and beauty in this enchanted woodland.

A Place You Must See

Tenerife's Laurel Forest is a must-see location for eco-tourists, wildlife lovers, and anybody looking for a peaceful getaway. You may re-establish a connection with nature, rediscover inner serenity, and learn about the marvels of the natural world here thanks to its beauty, biodiversity, and enthralling environment.

7. Vacation via Afur-Cruz de Carmen's Serene Landscapes

Tucked away in the lush hills of Anaga, the northeasternmost mountain range in Tenerife, is the fascinating Afur-Cruz de Carmen hiking path, which reveals the island's scenic splendor and rich cultural legacy. Trekking through a varied environment of lush woods, volcanic formations, and charming communities, this moderately tough trek offers hikers of all skill levels an insight into Tenerife's fascinating natural treasures and rich history.

Overview of Trail

- Dimensions: 6.5 km (4 miles)
- Secondary Time: 3–4 hours
- Moderate in difficulty
- Ancient Elevation: 1,794 feet or 550 meters

Point of origin:

The walk starts in the quaint seaside hamlet of Afur, which has traditional architecture and a rich historical background. There is plenty of parking in the village.

Description of Route:

The walk begins in Afur and climbs slowly through a beautiful forest of laurisilva, the famous laurisilva that forms the distinctive Anaga mountain of Tenerife. The lovely smell of laurel leaves and the melodic sounds of birds fill the air, offering a much-needed break from the heat in the forest.

Ascending farther will bring you to the Cruz de Carmen, a well-known monument with expansive views of the surroundings. An emblem of religion and custom, the cross bears witness to the religious legacy of the island.

The route continues beyond the Cruz de Carmen via a sequence of hills and ravines formed by volcanic eruptions, offering breath-taking vistas of the Atlantic Ocean and the Anaga Mountains. The environment is given a dramatic touch by the jagged rocks and contrasting colors of the volcanic region.

Many little towns, including Chamorga and Roque Negro, will pass by along the route where you may stop and experience the warmth of the locals. These communities, with their whitewashed buildings, winding lanes, and welcoming locals, provide an insight into Tenerife's traditional way of life.

After there, the route descends into the settlement of Afur while going past terraced hills and farmland. A panoramic view of the settlement, the coast, and the nearby islands of La Gomera and La Palma may be seen throughout the descent.

Protective Measures:

- Don't forget to pack lots of water and sunscreen, and wear supportive hiking shoes.
- If it has been raining, use caution as the track might become slick.
- Exercise care on the trail's steeper parts and be aware of the uneven ground.
- Be mindful of the surrounding environment and remove any signs of your visit.

Further Advice:

- To avoid the heat, start your walk early in the morning if you're going during the summer.

- You may have a little lunch or snack at one of Afur's many cafés and eateries.
- Carry a camera to record the breathtaking vistas as you travel the path.

Hiking the Afur-Cruz de Carmen walk is a fascinating experience that combines cultural history, scenic vistas, and natural beauty. It is the ideal option for hikers of all skill levels looking for an amazing journey in Tenerife because of its moderate difficulty and varied sceneries.

8. Cruz del Carmen-Punta del Hidalgo

Adventurers are drawn to the Cruz del Carmen-Punta del Hidalgo path, which is tucked away within the lush surroundings of Tenerife's Anaga massif. The trek boasts of stunning vistas, a wide variety of flora and animals, and a hint of historical importance. A view into Tenerife's rich natural heritage and cultural tapestry, this moderately strenuous walk spans roughly 6.5

kilometers (4 miles) and takes you through a beautiful tapestry of lush woods, volcanic formations, and picturesque communities.

Overview of Trail
- Dimensions:** 6.5 km (4 miles)
- Secondary Time:** 3–4 hours
- Moderate in difficulty
- Ancient Elevation: 1,794 feet or 550 meters

Point of origin:

The walk starts in the sleepy town of Afur, a historical seaside community with traditional architecture. You may leave your car in the village and start your hiking trip since there is plenty of parking available.

Description of Route:

The route begins at Afur and climbs slowly through a lush field of laurel trees, the famous laurisilva that typifies Tenerife's Anaga mountain. The fragrant aroma of laurel leaves and the melodic sounds of birdsong fill the air, offering a much-needed break from the heat of the sun.

The Cruz de Carmen is a notable monument that bears witness to the island's religious legacy as you continue your journey. Situated atop a hill, the cross provides sweeping views of the surrounding terrain, extending beyond the Anaga Mountains and into the glittering Atlantic Ocean.

The route heads into a region of volcanic hills and ravines from the Cruz de Carmen, offering spectacular views of the Atlantic Ocean and the Anaga Mountains. You are left in awe of nature's artistic ability by the dramatic touch of the volcanic environment, which has jagged rocks and contrasting colors.

You will travel through a number of quaint towns along the road, such as Chamorga and Roque

Negro, where you may stop, enjoy some local cuisine, and get a taste of the island's customs. These communities provide a window into Tenerife's essence with its whitewashed homes, winding alleyways, and kind locals.

After there, the route dips in the direction of Punta del Hidalgo, a peaceful coastal community renowned for its lovely beaches and calm ambiance. A picture-perfect background to your incredible voyage awaits you as you descend, rewarding you with expansive views of the hamlet, the shoreline, and the nearby islands of La Gomera and La Palma.

Protective Measures:
- Be ready for the weather: Since the weather in the mountains may change quickly, always bring lots of water and sunscreen.
- Be mindful of your footing: In rainy weather, the route may be slick, so proceed with care, particularly on steep parts.

- Preserve the environment: Make sure to properly dispose of rubbish and leave no evidence of your visit.
- Ask for help if needed: Do not be afraid to ask other hikers or the local authorities for assistance if you run into any problems.

Further Advice:

- Organize your walk: Before heading out, check the trail conditions and weather prediction.
- Pack appropriately: Protect yourself from the sun by dressing comfortably, packing a hat, and wearing sturdy hiking boots.
- Embrace the journey: Go slowly, notice the beauty of the surroundings, and use your camera to record moments.
- Participate in sustainability: Show your support for regional companies, buy eco-friendly goods, and take care of the environment.

Hiking the Cruz del Carmen-Punta del Hidalgo path is a captivating experience that combines breathtaking scenery, cultural history, and the beauty of the natural world. It is the ideal option for hikers of all skill levels looking for an amazing journey in Tenerife because of its moderate difficulty and varied sceneries. So grab your spirit of adventure, lace on your boots, and set off to explore the lush scenery and quaint towns that lie ahead on this alluring path.

9. The Afur-Chamorga Trail

Adventurers are drawn to the Afur-Chamorga path, which is tucked away among the lush slopes of Tenerife's Anaga massif. The trek offers stunning vistas, a variety of flora and animals, and a hint of historical importance. A view into Tenerife's rich natural heritage and cultural fabric, this moderately strenuous walk spans around 4 kilometers (2.5 miles) and winds through a beautiful tapestry of lush woods, volcanic formations, and picturesque communities.

Overview of Trail

- Distance: 2.5 miles/4 km
- Time: two to three hours
- Moderate in difficulty
- Ancient Elevation: 1,148 feet or 350 meters

Point of origin:

The walk starts in the sleepy town of Afur, a historical seaside community with traditional architecture. You may leave your car in the village and start your hiking trip since there is plenty of parking available.

Description of Route:

The route begins at Afur and climbs slowly through a lush field of laurel trees, the famous laurisilva that typifies Tenerife's Anaga mountain. The fragrant aroma of laurel leaves and the melodic sounds of birdsong fill the air, offering a much-needed break from the heat of the sun.

You will be rewarded with expansive vistas of the Atlantic Ocean and the shimmering Anaga Mountains as you continue your journey. The route offers amazing views of the surroundings as it goes through a sequence of hills and ravines formed by volcanic activity. You are left in awe of nature's artistic ability by the dramatic touch of the volcanic environment, which has jagged rocks and contrasting colors.

You will go via the quaint town of Chamorga, which is tucked away within a verdant landscape. Take a vacation, indulge in regional cuisine, and get fully immersed in the customs of the island. The town provides a window into the spirit of Tenerife with its whitewashed homes, winding lanes, and kind locals.

After that, the route winds through a lush woodland, providing a peaceful haven from the outer world. A wide range of fauna, including the buzzard and the Tenerife lizard, find a home in the rich foliage, which is home to ferns, mosses, and other indigenous flora.

You will return to Afur at the trail's finish, having gained a fresh respect for the island's scenic splendor and rich cultural legacy. Pause to think back on your trip and relish the memories you have made thus far.

Protective Measures:

- Be ready for the weather: Since the weather in the mountains may change quickly, always bring lots of water and sunscreen.
- Be mindful of your footing: In rainy weather, the route may be slick, so proceed with care, particularly on steep parts.

- Preserve the environment: Make sure to properly dispose of rubbish and leave no evidence of your visit.
- Ask for help if needed: Do not be afraid to ask other hikers or the local authorities for assistance if you run into any problems.

Further Advice:

- Organize your walk: Before heading out, check the trail conditions and weather prediction.
- Pack appropriately: Protect yourself from the sun by dressing comfortably, packing a hat, and wearing sturdy hiking boots.
- Embrace the journey: Go slowly, notice the beauty of the surroundings, and use your camera to record moments.
- Participate in sustainability: Show your support for regional companies, buy eco-friendly goods, and take care of the environment.

Hiking the Afur-Chamorga path is a magical experience that combines breathtaking scenery, cultural legacy, and the beauty of the natural world. It is the ideal option for hikers of all skill levels looking for an amazing journey in Tenerife because of its moderate difficulty and varied sceneries. So grab your spirit of adventure, lace on your boots, and set off to explore the lush scenery and quaint towns that lie ahead on this alluring path.

10. Igueste-Semaforo

The "Island of Eternal Spring," Tenerife, is home to several hiking paths that highlight the island's distinctive volcanic scenery and varied ecosystems. Hiking the Igueste-Semaforo-Taganana-Chamorga path is a demanding but rewarding experience that offers stunning views of the island and beyond as well as a range of terrains, from verdant woods to desolate volcanic landscapes.

Tenerife hiking guide

Overview of Trail
- Length: 7.2 miles or 11.6 km
- Length: 6–8 hours
- Difficulty: Struggly
- A gain of 1,194 meters (3,917 ft) in elevation

Point of origin:

About 25 km from the town of La Orotava, in the hamlet of Igueste de San Andrés, is where the path starts. There is parking close to the trailhead.

Description of Route:

The trail's first ascent through a pine grove provides a pleasant break from the heat. You will leave the woodland and reach a desolate volcanic environment as you ascend higher. This portion of the hike offers just stunning vistas.

You will arrive at the Altavista Mountain Refuge, a well-liked location for hikers to stop and replenish, after traveling around 3 km. Because the refuge is 3,550 meters (11,647 feet) above sea level, you should adjust to the altitude before proceeding.

The path leads upwards from the Altavista Mountain Refuge to the top of Spain's tallest mountain, Mount Teide. The hardest part of the path is the last stretch, which has loose scree and steep inclines. But every step is worthwhile because of the sights at the summit.

You will be rewarded with expansive views over Tenerife, the nearby islands of La Gomera, La Palma, and El Hierro, and on a clear day, even the peak of Mount Atlas in Morocco, after you reach the top of Mount Teide. Spend some time admiring the scenery and relishing your sense of achievement.

The path for the descent and climb is the same. On the loose screen, take your time and use caution.

Protective Measures:

- Don't forget to pack lots of water and sunscreen, and wear supportive hiking footwear.
- If it has been raining, use caution as the walk may become slick.
- Before trekking, make sure you acclimatize yourself since the altitude might be high in certain places.
- Pace yourself and take breaks when necessary since the latter half of the trek may be rather difficult.
- You may want to think about going on a shorter or easier walk if your physical health isn't too great.
- Since the weather on the mountain may change quickly, make sure to check the weather prediction before you go.

Further Advice:

- To avoid the heat, start your walk early in the morning if you're going during the summer.
- Refreshments are available at the trailhead's little café.
- Carry a camera to record the breathtaking vistas as you travel the path.

Hiking the Igueste-Semaforo-Taganana-Chamorga path is a demanding but rewarding way to reach the top of one of the most famous volcanoes in the world. It is an absolute must-do for every hiker visiting Tenerife, because of its stunning vistas and varied landscapes.

11. Taganana - Chamorga

Situated in the lush surroundings of Tenerife's Anaga mountain, the Taganana-Chamorga path entices hikers with its assurance of stunning vistas, a varied array of flora and animals, and a hint of historical importance. A view into Tenerife's rich natural heritage and cultural fabric, this moderately strenuous walk spans around 5 kilometers (3.1 miles) and takes you through a beautiful tapestry of lush woods, impressive volcanic formations, and attractive communities.

Trail Summary
- Length: 3.1 miles or 5 km
- Two to three hours
- Moderate in difficulty
- Gain in Altitude: 250 meters (820 feet)

Beginning Point:
The peaceful community of Taganana, a seaside paradise renowned for its gorgeous beaches and calm environment, is where the route starts. You may leave your car in the village and start your trekking trip since parking is provided there.

Route Synopsis:

The path leaves Taganana and climbs gradually through a lush grove of laurisilva, the characteristic laurisilva of Tenerife's Anaga mountain. The fragrant aroma of laurel leaves and the melodic sounds of birdsong fill the air, offering a much-needed break from the heat of the sun.

You will be rewarded with expansive vistas of the Atlantic Ocean and the shimmering Anaga Mountains as you continue your journey. The route offers amazing views of the surroundings as it goes through a sequence of hills and ravines formed by volcanic activity. You are left in awe of nature's artistic ability by the dramatic touch of the volcanic environment, which has jagged rocks and contrasting colors.

You will travel through a number of quaint towns along the road, such as Roque Negro and Benijo, where you may stop, enjoy some local cuisine, and get a taste of the island's customs. These communities provide a window into Tenerife's essence with its whitewashed homes, winding alleyways, and kind locals.

After that, the route winds through a lush woodland, providing a peaceful haven from the outer world. A wide range of fauna, including the buzzard and the Tenerife lizard, find a home in the rich foliage, which is home to ferns, mosses, and other indigenous flora.

After finishing the path, you'll arrive in Chamorga, a charming town surrounded by thick nature. Before you go back to your starting place, pause to see the charming folks and their historic architecture.

Safety Measures:
- Always pack extra water and sunscreen in case the weather changes quickly in the mountains. Be ready for everything.

- Be mindful of your footing: In rainy weather, the terrain may be slick, so take extra care, particularly on steep parts.
- Treat the environment with respect by removing all traces of your presence and properly disposing of rubbish.
- Ask for help when you need it: If you run into any problems, don't be afraid to ask other hikers or the local authorities for assistance.

Extra Advice:

- Plan your walk: Before heading out, check the trail conditions and the weather prediction.
- Pack sensibly: Protect yourself from the sun by wearing a hat, cozy clothes, and strong hiking boots.
- Accept the journey: Go slowly, take in the scenery, and use your camera to record special moments.

- Encourage sustainability by using eco-friendly items, patronizing nearby companies, and showing consideration for the environment.

Hiking the Taganana-Chamorga route is a magical experience that combines breathtaking scenery, cultural legacy, and natural beauty. It is the ideal option for hikers of all skill levels looking for an amazing journey in Tenerife because of its moderate difficulty and varied sceneries. So grab your spirit of adventure, lace on your boots, and set off to explore the lush scenery and quaint towns that lie ahead on this alluring path.

12. Masca Gorge

Tucked down in the rough terrain of Tenerife's Teno Mountains, the Masca Gorge is a striking example of the strength and beauty of the natural world. A must-visit location for daring hikers and nature lovers alike, this stunning ravine, sculpted by ancient volcanic activity, provides an exhilarating trek through a region of towering cliffs, dense foliage, and hidden waterfalls.

An Account of Volcanic Causes

The Masca Gorge was created by volcanic eruptions that altered Tenerife's terrain millions of years ago. Lava flows formed a steep-sided canyon with a maximum elevation of 1,476 feet and a valley below, resulting from its solidification and erosion.

An Exciting Trek Waits

A somewhat strenuous walk leads into the center of this geological marvel on the Masca Gorge path. Starting from the town of Masca, the walk winds its way down into the valley, providing amazing views of the high cliffs of the ravine and the verdant flora that clings to its flanks.

A sequence of waterfalls will come into view as you proceed further down the canyon; they tumble down the steep hillsides and provide a symphony of sound and vision. The surrounding foliage contributes to the peaceful ambiance, and the cold water offers a nice break from the heat of the day.

A Sanctuary of Biodiversity

In addition to being a wonder of geology, the Masca Gorge is a wildlife sanctuary. With its protected valleys and copious amounts of rainfall, the gorge's distinct microclimate fosters a wide variety of plant and animal life.

Amid the luxuriant foliage, endemic flora flourish, like the huge Canary Island laurel and the Canary Island heather. The Tenerife kestrel and Berthelot's pipit are only two of the many bird species that call the valley home, contributing to its allure.

Exploration via Discovery

Trekking through the Masca Gorge is an experiential adventure that entails more than simply physical exertion. Spend some time admiring the beautiful flowers, the fascinating rock formations, and the brilliant colors of the surrounding area while you hike.

Take a moment to enjoy the sounds of nature, such as cascading waterfalls, rustling leaves, and chirping birds. Allow the beauty of nature to enchant your senses as you lose yourself in the peace and quiet of the gorge.

A Reminder of the Majesty of Nature

You'll be met with expansive vistas of the surrounding countryside that reach all the way to the Atlantic Ocean when you emerge from the Masca Gorge. Your feeling of achievement and the breathtaking surroundings will give you a fresh perspective on the grandeur of nature.

Adventure and breathtaking scenery come together at the Masca Gorge. This is a location where you may push your physical limits, take in the beauty of the natural environment, and make lifelong memories. So grab your sense of awe, lace on your boots, and get ready for an incredible voyage into the Masca Gorge's depths.

13. Monte del Agua's Enchanting Realm

Situated in the beautiful hillsides of Tenerife's Anaga massif, Monte del Agua entices those who love the outdoors with views of lush woods, stunning volcanic formations, and a hint of cultural legacy. A view into Tenerife's rich natural beauty and cultural fabric, this moderately tough trek spans around 8 km (5 miles) and winds through a stunning tapestry of laurisilva woods, volcanic ravines, and small communities.

Laurasilva's Sanctuary
The walk starts in the quaint seaside hamlet of Erjos, which is renowned for its traditional architecture and rich history. You will be met as you go by a lush field of laurel trees, the famous laurisilva that makes up Tenerife's Anaga mountain. With their complex branches and evergreen foliage, these old trees create a canopy that blocks out sunlight and fosters a calm and peaceful environment.

A Domain of Volcanic Structures

The path offers spectacular views of the Anaga Mountains and the Atlantic Ocean as it passes through a succession of volcanic ravines and hills. You are left in awe of nature's artistic ability by the dramatic touch of the volcanic environment, which has jagged rocks and contrasting colors.

A View Into Conventional Living

You'll travel through a number of quaint towns along the road, such as Tierra de Trigo and Las Portelas, where you can stop, enjoy some local cuisine, and get a taste of the island's customs. These communities provide a window into Tenerife's essence with its whitewashed homes, winding alleyways, and kind locals.

A Refuge for Animals

A wide variety of flora and fauna may be found at Monte del Agua. Look out for the buzzard, a flying bird of prey that soars above the forest canopy, and the Tenerife lizard, a little, nimble species that lounges in the sun on rocks.

A Trip of Inquiry and Meditation

Hiking at Monte del Agua is a contemplative and self-discovery experience rather than only a physical hike. Spend some time admiring the trail's dense laurel woods, striking volcanic rocks, and quaint settlements scattered across the scenery.

Take Comfort in the Quiet

Take a moment to appreciate the sounds of nature: the rustling of leaves, the chirping of birds, and the soft whisper of the wind among the trees. Take in the peace and quiet of the woodland and let your senses be enthralled by the beauty of nature.

A Fulfilling Adventure

You will be rewarded with expansive vistas of the surrounding terrain when you reach the horizon after finishing your walk. Your feeling of success and the breathtaking surroundings will give you a fresh perspective on the grandeur of nature.

A location where adventure and breathtaking scenery come together is Monte del Agua. This is a location where you may push your physical limits, take in the beauty of the natural environment, and make lifelong memories. So prepare for an incredible excursion into the enchanted world of Monte del Agua, a genuine treasure of Tenerife's natural heritage. Lace up your boots and carry a feeling of awe.

14. Los Cristianos to Teno Alto

Tucked away on the southwest coast of Tenerife, Los Cristianos entices visitors with its dynamic atmosphere, sun-kissed beaches, and rich cultural legacy. Set off on an incredible adventure from this vibrant resort town to Teno Alto, a peaceful mountain community brimming with old world charm and stunning natural beauty. This walk, which is somewhat difficult and covers around 6.5 kilometers (4 miles), provides a stunning combination of coastline views, lush woods, and volcanic formations, giving visitors an insight into Tenerife's varied landscapes and cultural mosaic.

An Oceanfront Preface
The trip starts at Los Cristianos Beach, a charming expanse of golden sand that is kissed by the Atlantic Ocean's turquoise waves. Before you go on your trip, pause to enjoy the sun-drenched ambiance, the soothing cadence of the waves, and the energetic bustle of the seaside promenade.

Climbing Up the Verde
The route softly rises into the lush hills of the Anaga Massif as you leave the busy tourist town behind.

The terrain changes to a tapestry of verdant laurisilva woods, the quintessential laurisilva of Tenerife's natural heritage. A calm, peaceful environment is produced by the old trees' evergreen foliage and complex branches, which create a canopy that absorbs the sunshine.

With its stunning views of the Anaga Mountains and the glittering Atlantic Ocean, the path meanders through a succession of volcanic ravines and hills. You are left in awe of nature's artistic ability by the dramatic touch of the volcanic environment, which has jagged rocks and contrasting colors.

A Hint of Convention

The little town of Roque Negro, a refuge of classic architecture and gracious hospitality, will pass you by on the route. Take a moment to indulge in regional specialties, such as the delicious papas con mojo, and get fully immersed in the rich cultural legacy of the island. Tenerife's heart and soul may be seen in the village's whitewashed buildings, winding alleyways, and kind locals.

A Refuge for Animals
Many different kinds of plants and animals may be found in the trail's refuge. Look out for the buzzard, a flying bird of prey that soars above the forest canopy, and the Tenerife lizard, a little, nimble species that lounges in the sun on rocks.

A Path of Inquiry and Meditation
The walk from Los Cristianos to Teno Alto is a voyage of introspection and self-discovery as much as a physical ascent. Spend some time admiring the trail's dense laurel woods, striking volcanic rocks, and quaint settlements scattered across the scenery.

Accept the Quietness
Take a moment to appreciate the sounds of nature: the rustling of leaves, the chirping of birds, and the soft whisper of the wind among the trees. Let the

beauties of nature enthrall your senses as you lose yourself in the peace and quiet of the natural world.

An Exciting Place to Go

You will feel a feeling of success when arriving at Teno Alto, and the breathtaking scenery will inspire a fresh admiration for the grandeur of nature. Teno Alto, with its whitewashed cottages, winding alleyways, and stunning panoramic vistas, is a peaceful haven from the bustle of the coast, nestled among the craggy peaks of the Teno Mountains.

A Site of Exploration

Discover the village's historic architecture, pause to enjoy the regional food, and interact with the amiable locals, who will be happy to share their customs and tales.

An Unforgettable Trip

The trip from Los Cristianos to Teno Alto combines the natural beauty of the coast, lush surroundings, and rich cultural legacy, making it an amazing experience. You'll come away from this trip with a profound respect for Tenerife's natural beauties and its kind people. Put on your boots, gather your spirit of adventure, and set off on a voyage that will leave you with priceless memories.

15. Erjos

The community of Erjos, which is tucked away among the lush slopes of Tenerife's Anaga ridge, entices visitors with its ageless appeal, extensive agricultural legacy, and stunning natural settings. Situated at an elevation of more than 900 meters (2,953 feet), this peaceful refuge transports you to a world of beautiful scenery and genuine island customs, providing a pleasant break from the busy coastal resorts.

A Trip Through Time

The native Tenerife people known as the Guanches are the source of Erjos. The village's name, which is a play on the Guanche term "," which means "ravine," refers to the network of volcanic ravines that surround it.

Erjos has contributed significantly to Tenerife's agricultural environment throughout the ages. The community has traditionally encouraged the growth of a range of crops, including potatoes, beans, and chestnuts, because of its good soil and mild environment. Erjos was also well-known, until recently, for its vast network of "minas de tierra," or earth mines, from which volcanic soil was taken for use in building and agriculture.

A Natural Beauty Haven

A mosaic of rich vegetation envelops Erjos, including the recognisable laurisilva forest, which is recognised as a UNESCO World Heritage Site. These old woods, which are distinguished by their mosses, ferns, and evergreen trees, provide a home for a wide variety of plant and animal species and foster a serene, lush ambiance.

The village's natural beauty is further enhanced by its closeness to the Anaga Rural Park, a protected natural area. Trekking paths meander around the park, providing stunning vistas of the shimmering Atlantic Ocean and the Anaga Mountains.

A Textile of Cultures

Here in Erjos, modernism and tradition coexist together. The village's tiny lanes and whitewashed cottages give off an air of old world beauty, and its residents still engage in time-honored customs like artisanal crafts and farming.

The community puts on colorful displays of regional culture, music, and dance during its yearly fiestas, which include the Fiesta de San Isidro and the Fiesta del Rosario. These festivities provide a window into Erjos's essence, exhibiting the friendliness and hospitality of its populace.

A Haven of Peace and Exploration

For those looking for a peaceful getaway and a closer relationship with nature, Erjos is the perfect place to visit. Erjos is the perfect place to unwind and revitalize, whether you're trekking through the lush woods, discovering the village's quaint alleys, or just taking in the tranquil ambiance.

So explore the area beyond the busy shore and take in Erjos's true appeal. Explore a community where natural beauty coexists with tradition; you'll leave with a deep respect for Tenerife's rich history and the peace of its natural treasures.

16. Santiago del Teide to Masca

The track from Santiago del Teide to Masca, which blends spectacular natural beauty with a dash of adventure, provides an amazing hiking experience. It is tucked away within the untamed landscapes of Tenerife's Teno Mountains. This rather strenuous path, about 4.5 km (2.8 miles) long, leads you through an intriguing fusion of volcanic peaks, lush woods, and undiscovered waterfalls before arriving at the spectacular Masca Gorge.

A Tour across Volcanic Environments
The walk starts in the peaceful community of Santiago del Teide, a little retreat renowned for its historic buildings and kind hosts. The untamed beauty of the Teno Mountains awaits you as you begin your walk, serving as a reminder of the strong volcanic forces that sculpted Tenerife's topography.

The route offers amazing views of the surrounding peaks and the glittering Atlantic Ocean in the distance as it passes through a succession of volcanic ravines and hills. You are left in awe of nature's artistic ability by the dramatic touch of the volcanic environment, which has jagged rocks and contrasting colors.

A Paradise of Greenery and Secret Treasures

When you keep going up, you'll come across a lush area of laurisilva woodland, which are the famous laurel woods of Tenerife's Anaga Mountains. With their complex branches and evergreen foliage, these old trees create a canopy that blocks out sunlight and fosters a calm and peaceful environment.

Look for hidden waterfalls that provide a refreshing break from the heat of the sun with their refreshing waters trickling down the rocky hillsides. The sound of rustling leaves and birdsong enhances the peacefulness of the forest, resulting in a fully immersive encounter with nature.

A Lowering Into the Masca Canyon

Eventually, the route dips into the stunning Masca Gorge, a chasm sculpted by long-ago volcanic activity. The gorge offers breathtaking views of the towering cliffs and thick flora that clings to its sides as it plunges over 450 meters (1,476 feet) to the valley below.

Take time to enjoy the beautiful flowers, exquisite rock formations, and vivid colors of the surrounding area as you make your way across the rocky terrain and small walkways. The Masca Gorge is a site that will inspire and humble you, and it is a monument to the strength and beauty of nature.

A Fulfilling Achievement
As soon as you emerge from the Masca Gorge, you'll feel a feeling of achievement and a fresh appreciation for the grandeur of nature. As you gaze out over the stunning scenery that stretches all the way to the Atlantic Ocean, your amazing journey will live on in your memory.

Hiking combines adventure, scenic beauty, and cultural legacy on its route from Santiago del Teide to Masca. It serves as a reminder of the world-changing potential of nature, the value of conservation, and the excitement of seeing the globe on foot. So grab your sense of curiosity, put on your boots, and set off on an incredible trek across the untamed terrain of Tenerife's Teno Mountains.

17. La Caldera de Taburiente:

La Caldera de Taburiente National Park, tucked away among the untamed vistas of Tenerife's central highlands, is a monument to the strength and splendor of nature. This enormous caldera provides a unique combination of striking vistas, varied ecosystems, and a rich cultural legacy. It was created by a massive volcanic explosion millions of years ago.

A Wonder of Geology

One of the biggest calderas on Earth, La Caldera de Taburiente, also known as "The Caldera of Taburiente" in Spanish, is about 10 kilometers (6.2

miles) in diameter and descends more than 2,400 meters (7,874 feet) from the rim to the valley floor. Scientists and explorers have been enthralled by this enormous crater, which was created when a massive volcano collapsed, for millennia.

A Landscape Tapestry

As you descend into the caldera, you'll be met with an enthralling tapestry of landscapes, each with an own personality. Magnificent karst formations, like the well-known Roque Cinchado, with their sharp peaks extending to the heavens, serve as quiet guardians. The slopes are covered with dense pine woods, which provide a lush contrast to the volcanic environment.

Deep ravines are carved out by the chilly waters of waterfalls that tumble down stony cliffs. Ancient lava flows dot the caldera floor, their cemented surfaces serving as a testament to the strong forces that sculpted the surrounding terrain.

A Biodiversity Haven

La Caldera de Taburiente National Park is home to a wide variety of plant and animal species, making it a sanctuary for biodiversity. With its diverse ecosystems and copious amounts of rain, the park's distinct microclimate fosters a thriving ecology that has adapted to flourish in this paradise of volcanic eruptions.

Color splashes are added to the scene by endemic flora like the dainty retama broom and the massive Canary Island laurel. The sounds of singing birds, such as the Tenerife kestrel and the Berthelot's pipit, fill the sky as they fly over the heavens.

A Legacy of Culture

For millennia, people have lived at La Caldera de Taburiente, and the park is replete with reminders of this rich cultural past. Archaeological sites provide insights into the life of the island's original inhabitants. One such site is the ancient Guanche village of La Guancha.

Nestled in the slopes of the caldera, traditional communities provide a window into the island's pastoral way of life. The local customs, handicrafts, and food all reflect the vibrant cultural legacy of the park.

A Discovery Journey
Discovering the marvels of nature and the depth of culture may be experienced by traveling through La Caldera de Taburiente National Park. Explore lush woods, take in the sight of striking volcanic structures, and find undiscovered waterfalls.

Talk to the welcoming park visitors, discover their customs, and enjoy the tastes of regional food. Think about the strength of nature, the value of conservation, and the lasting impact of human presence in this unique setting as you explore.

There is a convergence of adventure, natural beauty, and cultural history in La Caldera de Taburiente National Park. This serves as a poignant reminder of the transformational power of nature, the need to protect the planet's delicate ecosystems, and the pleasure that comes from forging connections with the land and its people. Put on your boots, gather your sense of awe, and set off on an incredible excursion into Tenerife's interior.

17. La Corona

Tucked down among the craggy peaks of Tenerife's Teno Mountains, La Corona Viewpoint is a magnificent example of the creativity of nature. At a height of around 750 meters (2,461 feet), this charming viewpoint provides an amazing view of Tenerife's northwest coast, the Orotava Valley, and the island's most impressive feature, Mount Teide.

A Trip to an Ecological Refuge

Traveling to La Corona Viewpoint is a unique trip. A meandering road winds up through a tapestry of lush greenery from the little community of La Guancha, providing views of the surrounding area as you climb higher. As you go closer to the vantage point, the air becomes crisper and colder, and your excitement builds with each step.

You'll be met with an unmatched sight of unspoiled natural splendor as soon as you arrive at the viewpoint. Spreading out before you like a lush carpet, the Orotava Valley is home to charming towns, lush farms, and the famous Pyramids of Güímar, a group of volcanic cones that lend an air of mystique to the surroundings.

An Unfurled Painter's Palette

Tenerife's northwest coast opens like a palette for a painter, with colors ranging from the delicate greens of the coastal plains to the vivid blues of the Atlantic Ocean. The top peak of Tenerife, Mount Teide, rises majestically in the distance, its snow-capped crown penetrating the blue sky.

The scenery becomes a work of light and shadow art as the sun casts red and gold colors over the sky. As the sun sets, the colors of the Orotava Valley are accentuated by the contrast with the mountains that are becoming darker. The enchanting lights of far-off towns provide a magical quality to the landscape.

A Refuge for Exploration Seekers

La Corona Viewpoint is a gathering area for thrill-seekers as well as a site for contemplative viewing. From this perspective, hang-gliders and paragliders take off, gliding smoothly over the valley with their colorful wings standing out against the vastness of the sky.

Hiking and exploring options abound on the nearby paths, which wind through lush woods, dramatic volcanic formations, and undiscovered waterfalls. The experience is enhanced by the exhilarating air and the excitement of discovery.

A Place of Refuge for the Senses

The La Corona Viewpoint is a sensory haven. The pleasant aroma of wildflowers wafts in the mild wind, birdsong reverberates through the air, and the sound of rustling leaves frames the tranquil sounds of the natural world. The panoramic view enthralls the sight and evokes awe and wonder in the spirit with its symphony of colors and textures.

A Priceless Find

La Corona Viewpoint has long been a popular destination for pilgrims, drawing both tourists and locals with its promise of breath-taking vistas and an intimate encounter with the majesty of nature.

It's a priceless find that will stay forever in the hearts and thoughts of all who visit, when Tenerife's splendorous beauty is shown.

So go to La Corona Viewpoint and experience the magnificence that lies ahead. Allow the breathtaking views to astound you, the fresh air to arouse your senses, and the peace of the surroundings to calm your spirit. Long after you've climbed down from the heights, the experience will stay with you as a reminder of the beauty of nature and its transformational power.

18. Chamorga-La Caldera

Tucked away in the rocky Anaga Massif of Tenerife, Chamorga-La Caldera is a magical place with lush woods, amazing volcanic formations, and undiscovered waterfalls. A beautiful tapestry of laurisilva woods, volcanic ravines, and flowing waterfalls can be found on this moderately strenuous 4-kilometer (2.5-mile) walk, which culminates in the stunning La Caldera, a collapsed volcano crater.

A Tour through the Enchanting Laurasilva

The walk starts in Chamorga, a peaceful community renowned for its traditional architecture and friendly people. The cold, crisp air of the Laurisilva woodland, a UNESCO World Heritage Site, will welcome you as you begin your walk. A wide variety of plant and animal species may be found living in these old woods, which are distinguished by their evergreen trees, ferns, and mosses. These forests also produce a calm and lush ambiance.

The path offers beautiful views of the Anaga Mountains and the glittering Atlantic Ocean in the distance as it passes through a succession of volcanic hills and ravines. You are left in awe of nature's artistic ability by the dramatic touch of the volcanic environment, which has jagged rocks and contrasting colors.

A Waterfall Symphony

A succession of waterfalls with calm streams tumbling down the steep hillsides may be seen as you continue on the Chamorga-La Caldera trek. Your trip will seem a little more serene and rejuvenated thanks to the soft sound of the waterfalls and the light mist filling the air.

Take a moment to appreciate the symphony of noises produced by the cascading waterfalls, the rustling of leaves, and the melodic bird calls. Take in the peace and quiet of the woodland and let your senses be enthralled by the beauty of nature.

A Drop Below the Caldera

Eventually the road descends into La Caldera, an extinct volcanic crater that provides an insight into the immense forces that sculpted Tenerife's terrain. Many different plant and animal species may find a unique home in the crater because of its high walls and abundant flora.

Spend some time admiring the beautiful flowers, the complex rock formations, and the vivid colors of the surrounding area as you explore the crater. La Caldera is a destination that will inspire and humble you, and it is a monument to the strength and beauty of nature.

A Fulfilling Achievement

You'll feel a feeling of achievement and a fresh appreciation for the grandeur of nature when you emerge from La Caldera. As you gaze out over the stunning scenery that stretches all the way to the Atlantic Ocean, your amazing journey will live on in your memory.

The route from Chamorga-La Caldera combines adventure, scenic beauty, and cultural legacy. It serves as a reminder of the world-changing potential of nature, the value of conservation, and the excitement of seeing the globe on foot. So grab your sense of awe, lace up your boots, and set off on an incredible voyage through the magical world of Chamorga-La Caldera.

19. Tigaiga-Ravine

Tucked up among the verdant hillsides of Tenerife's Anaga Massif, the Tigaiga-Ravine of San Fernando is a magnificent example of the strength and splendor of the natural world. A must-visit location for daring hikers and nature lovers alike, this stunning ravine, sculpted by ancient volcanic activity, provides an exhilarating trek through a region of towering cliffs, dense foliage, and hidden waterfalls.

A Tour Through the Centre of the Anaga Massif

The town of San Fernando, a quaint retreat renowned for its traditional architecture and gracious hospitality, is where the trek to the Tigaiga-Ravine of San Fernando starts. You will be met by the cold, crisp air of the UNESCO World Heritage Site, the Anaga Massif, as you set out on your walk.

The walk offers amazing views of the cliff-like walls of the ravine and the verdant flora that clings to its sides as it weaves through a succession of volcanic ravines and hills. You are left in awe of nature's artistic ability by the dramatic touch of the volcanic environment, which has jagged rocks and contrasting colors.

A Paradise of Greenery and Secret Treasures

Following your descent into the ravine, you will enter a lush area of laurisilva woodland, which are the recognisable laurel woods of Tenerife's Anaga Massif. With their complex branches and evergreen foliage, these old trees create a canopy that blocks out sunlight and fosters a calm and peaceful environment.

Look for hidden waterfalls that provide a refreshing break from the heat of the sun with their refreshing waters trickling down the rocky hillsides. The sound of rustling leaves and birdsong enhances the peacefulness of the forest, resulting in a fully immersive encounter with nature.

A Symphony of Calm and Waterfalls

There are several tumbling waterfalls in San Fernando's Tigaiga-Ravine, each with its own distinct beauty and charm. In the middle of the valley, the Agua de Dios waterfall is a delightful refuge with its slow flow and cool mist.

Ascending the route further will bring you to the impressive El Salto waterfall, whose sheer drop produces an amazing sight. It's the perfect place to stop and take in the beauty of the surroundings since the waterfall's refreshing spray gives the air a lift.

Following your investigation, you'll come upon undiscovered waterfalls nestled among the foliage, their peaceful cascades blending into the natural harmony. The splendor of the ravine is seen from a different angle by each waterfall, which heightens the attractiveness of this magical place.

A Fulfilling Achievement

As you emerge from San Fernando's Tigaiga-Ravine, you'll feel a feeling of achievement and a fresh appreciation for the grandeur of nature.

The stunning vistas of the surrounding terrain that extend to the glittering Atlantic Ocean will linger in your memory as a memento of your amazing journey.

A walk through San Fernando's Tigaiga-Ravine offers a unique experience combining adventure, scenic beauty, and cultural legacy. It serves as a reminder of the world-changing potential of nature, the value of conservation, and the excitement of seeing the globe on foot. So grab your sense of awe, lace on your boots, and get ready for an amazing voyage into this enchanted ravine's depths.

20. La Ruleta

The "Circular Route of Los Cristianos," or La Ruleta, is a fascinating hiking track that leads you through a variety of varied landscapes on Tenerife's southwest coast. The route, which is around 10.5 kilometers (6.5 miles) long, provides a variety of coastline views, lush woods, and volcanic formations, giving visitors a taste of Tenerife's natural beauties and cultural legacy.

A Seaside Preface

The trip starts at Los Cristianos Beach, a charming expanse of golden sand that is kissed by the Atlantic Ocean's turquoise waves. Before you go on your trip, pause to enjoy the sun-kissed ambiance, the soothing rhythm of the waves, and the energetic bustle of the seaside promenade.

A Route via Verdant Villages

The route softly rises into the lush hills of the Anaga Massif as you leave the busy tourist town behind. The terrain changes to a tapestry of verdant laurisilva woods, the quintessential laurisilva of Tenerife's natural heritage.

A calm, peaceful environment is produced by the old trees' evergreen foliage and complex branches, which create a canopy that absorbs the sunshine. With its stunning views of the Anaga Mountains and the glittering Atlantic Ocean, the path meanders through a succession of volcanic ravines and hills.

You are left in awe of nature's artistic ability by the dramatic touch of the volcanic environment, which has jagged rocks and contrasting colors. The picturesque community of Roque Negro, a refuge of period architecture and gracious hospitality, is traversed along the path.

Take a moment to indulge in regional specialties, such as the delicious papas con mojo, and get fully immersed in the rich cultural legacy of the island. Tenerife's heart and soul may be seen in the village's whitewashed buildings, winding alleyways, and kind locals.

A View From Above

Arriving at the top of the Anaga Mountains, you are greeted with an amazing view. The Teno Mountains rise magnificently in the distance, their jagged peaks visible as the Atlantic Ocean spreads far into the horizon.

The setting is even more serene by the picturesque towns and lush valleys that dot the terrain. Allow the splendor of Tenerife to overwhelm your senses as you take a minute to capture this breathtaking scene with your camera.

A Drop Into Wonders of the Volcano

The route continues down through a sequence of hills and ravines formed by volcanic eruptions, providing a closer view of the remarkable volcanic structures that molded Tenerife's terrain. The Chayofita Barranco, a deep gorge surrounded by high rocks and rich flora, is traversed by the path.

Look out for unusual volcanic rock formations, such the well-known Roque Cinchado, a naturally occurring rock arch that demonstrates the strength of volcanic forces. Eventually, the route drops back down to the ocean, where the salty air and the sound of the waves welcome you back to Los Cristianos, a paradise for coastal residents.

4. HIKING ESSENTIALS

1. What to pack for a Tenerife hike

Tenerife is a wonderful island with dramatic coasts, rich woods, and volcanic landscapes. Hiking there provides an exciting combination of adventure and natural beauty. The secret to guaranteeing a safe and happy trip is preparation, whether you're hiking the lush paths of Anaga Massif or scaling the spectacular heights of Mount Teide. The following is a thorough packing suggestion for your hiking trip in Tenerife:

1. Dependable hiking boots:

Purchasing sturdy and comfortable hiking footwear is essential for tackling Tenerife's diverse landscapes. Choose footwear that can handle muddy treks and rough routes by providing ankle support, strong traction, and water resistance.

2. Breathable Gear for Hiking:

To adjust to Tenerife's varied weather, wear layers of clothing. To be comfortable while exerting yourself, choose for base layers that drain away sweat and dry quickly. For colder weather at higher elevations, use an insulating jacket or a lightweight fleece.

3. Wetsuit:
Because of Tenerife's erratic weather, expect unexpected downpours; thus, to be dry and safe, carry a lightweight rain jacket and waterproof trousers.

4. Sunscreen Use:
Because of Tenerife's subtropical climate, sunscreen is a must. To protect your skin and eyes from the sun's damaging rays, carry sunglasses, a wide-brimmed hat, and sunscreen with a high SPF.

5. Plenty of Water and Food:

Staying hydrated is essential to sustaining your energy levels when hiking. Keep a reusable water bottle with you and top it out often. To keep your body fuelled, pack energy-dense foods like dried fruits, granola bars, or trail mix.

6. Flashlight or headlamp:

A headlamp or torch is necessary for safe navigation if you want to walk at night or in poor light.

7. First Aid Package:

Have a basic first-aid kit on hand to handle minor cuts and injuries. Provide painkillers, bandages, antiseptic wipes, and blister care.

8. Viewfinder:

Take pictures or record the special moments from your hiking trip in Tenerife using a camera or smartphone.

9. Private Things:

Remember to bring along personal needs like a compact bag, trekking poles for extra stability, an emergency whistle and a map or GPS gadget for guidance.

10. Feeling of Wonder and a Positive Attitude:

Bring with plenty of energy, an open mind, and a profound respect for Tenerife's breathtaking natural surroundings.

Always keep in mind that having the appropriate equipment for your Tenerife hiking trip will guarantee you're ready to tackle the trails, rise to the difficulties, and make lifelong memories.

Tenerife Navigation:

The biggest and most populated of the Canary Islands, Tenerife, provides a captivating combination of sun-kissed beaches, verdant woods, and volcanic vistas. Tenerife has something for everyone, whether you're looking for quiet getaway, cultural immersion, or outdoor experiences. Understanding the many available transit choices is key to appreciating the island's variety and beauty to the fullest. With the help of this in-depth guide, you'll be able to travel Tenerife with ease and have a wonderful trip.

Departing Tenerife

With two international airports, Tenerife is easily accessible from a wide range of locations worldwide. The primary hub of the island, Tenerife South Airport (TFS), sometimes referred to as Reina Sofía Airport, is where most foreign aircraft land. Los Rodeos Airport, popularly known as Tenerife North Airport (TFN), is mostly used for internal and inter-island flights.

Traveling to Your Location:

There are several ways to go from the airports to different areas of Tenerife. Take into account these choices for a convenient and enjoyable travel:

- **Taxis**: Direct transportation to your accommodation or destination is provided by taxis, which are easily found outside both airports. Because they are metered, taxi charges are clear.

- **Public Buses:** Major cities and well-liked tourist attractions are connected by Tenerife's vast public bus network, TITSA. Travel planning tools and comprehensive timetables are available on the Titsa website and mobile app.

- **Renting a vehicle:** You can explore Tenerife at your own speed with freedom and flexibility when you rent a vehicle. There are a lot of automobile rental companies on the island as well as at the airports.

- **Excursions and Tours:** With the assistance of knowledgeable local guides, organized excursions and tours provide a convenient method to see certain parts of Tenerife. These trips often involve activities, food, and transportation.

How to Navigate Tenerife:
Once you've reached your location, a variety of transit alternatives make it simple to explore Tenerife's varied terrain and lively communities. Think about these choices for your island explorations:

- **Public Buses:** Major cities, villages, and tourist destinations are connected by TITSA's bus network, which stretches across the island. Buses are an inexpensive and practical mode of transportation.

- **Taxis**: The majority of towns and cities have taxis accessible, which provide a prompt and efficient form of transportation.

- **Car Rentals**: Hiring a vehicle is still a common way to see Tenerife's varied landscape and undiscovered attractions.

- **Hop-on-hop-off Tours**: With the option to get on and off at predetermined locations, these open-top buses provide a convenient way to see major cities and sites.

- **Ferry Services:** Tenerife and the nearby Canary Islands are connected by inter-island ferries, which makes it simple to explore the varied archipelago.

- **Walking and Hiking:** Tenerife has an extensive system of hiking paths that range in difficulty from leisurely strolls to strenuous climbs. Hiking and walking provide a comprehensive method to take in the island's natural splendor.

2. A Guide to Getting Around Tenerife:

Take into consideration these suggestions to guarantee a seamless and pleasurable travel experience in Tenerife:

- Arrange your schedule and travel requirements ahead of time.

- For convenience and cost savings, buy public transport tickets in advance.

- Learn the appropriate tipping amount and taxi etiquette.

- Give yourself enough time to travel, particularly during the busiest times of year.

- Be mindful of language difficulties and provide translation resources.

- Pay attention to the signage and traffic laws in your area.

Accept the relaxed pace of the island and enjoy the voyage.

Tenerife is waiting for you with its enthralling scenery, vibrant culture, and kind people. You'll be well-equipped to tour the island with ease if you comprehend the numerous transit alternatives and put these useful ideas to use. This will guarantee an amazing and fulfilling trip experience.

3. Leaving No Trace Principles :

Going into the wilderness gives you the opportunity to discover new places, get in touch with nature, and enjoy the peace and quiet of the great outdoors. But we must exercise caution and try to minimize our influence on these priceless habitats. By establishing a framework for ethical outdoor activity, the Leave No Trace (LNT) principles make sure that future generations may take in the same natural beauties that we do.

The Seven Principles of Leave No Trace:

1. Plan Ahead and Prepare: Careful preparation is necessary before starting any outdoor trip. Make sure you know the rules and conditions of the path, do some research on the place you want to visit, and bring the right supplies, clothes, and equipment.

2. Travel and Camp on Durable Surfaces: Whenever feasible, stay on designated trails and campgrounds. Steer clear of trail construction, trampled vegetation, and sensitive places such as meadows, shorelines, and archaeological sites while camping.

3. Reduce Waste: Take out all garbage, including leftover food, packaging, and feminine products. Trash should be disposed of correctly in approved containers or packed out for composting or recycling at home.

4. Leave What You Find: Refrain from gathering mementos made of plants, rocks, or animal artifacts. Save the environment's inherent beauty so that future generations may enjoy it.

5. Reduce the Impact of Campfires: If you want to utilize a campfire, build a small, enclosed fire pit or choose pre-existing fire rings. Use only fallen or dead wood, and make sure the fire is well out of control before you go.

6. Respect Wildlife: Keep a safe distance from wildlife and refrain from interfering with its natural activities. Avoid feeding animals since it may change their natural food sources and cause them to become reliant on people.

6. Take Care of Other Guests: Treat other people with respect and decency while using the trails and campgrounds. Be aware of noise levels, refrain from obstructing paths or monopolizing resources, and respect other guests' right to privacy and outdoor pleasure.

Further Advice on Leaving No Trace:

- To reduce waste, use reusable cups, cutlery, and water bottles.

Maintain good hygiene to safeguard water sources and stop the spread of illness.

- To preserve sensitive sites and prevent confrontations, abide by local laws and trail closures.

- Spread awareness of the Leave No Trace philosophy to encourage sensible outdoor leisure.

4. Hiking Etiquette:

Hiking provides an opportunity to physically push oneself, escape the daily grind, and take in the beauty of nature. But with outdoor activities becoming more and more popular, it's crucial now more than ever to walk responsibly. We can make sure that everyone enjoys their treks and that the trails are left as immaculate as when we discovered them by adhering to these rules.

Conserving the Environment of the Trail:

1. Remain on the Trail: To reduce harm to the environment and stop erosion, stick to authorized paths. Refrain from creating new paths or shortcuts.

2. Pack Out any garbage: Remove any leftover food, wrappers, and personal hygiene products from your garbage. Don't leave any evidence of your visit.

3. Carefully Dispose of rubbish: Pack out rubbish for recycling or composting at home, or use specially designated trash cans. Don't set rubbish on fire in the backcountry.

4. Reduce the Impact of Campfires: If you want to utilize a campfire, build a small, enclosed fire pit or choose pre-existing fire rings. Use only fallen or dead wood, and make sure the fire is well out of control before you go.

5. Preserve Water Sources: Steer clear of using water sources for dishwashing, tooth brushing, or personal hygiene. For these tasks, bring out water or use a special place for cleaning camp gear.

Caring for Wildlife:

1. Observe from a Distance: To prevent interfering with wildlife's natural behavior, observe from a safe distance. Don't feed or approach animals.

2. Keep Food Secure: To avoid attracting animals, store food appropriately in bear canisters or hanging from trees.

3. Respect Animal Homes: Refrain from going into or upsetting animal nests or dens. Leave fallen logs, rock formations, and other natural features unharmed.

4. Be Aware of Noise: Reduce noise levels to avoid upsetting animals or other hikers.

With Honour, Fellow Hikers:

1. Give Way to Uphill Hikers: Since they are hiking at a higher elevation, give way to them.

2. Be Courteous with Greetings: Give a nod or a courteous hello to other hikers.

3. Manage Your Dog: Make sure your dog is always on a leash and under control to avoid upsetting other hikers or animals.

4. Share the Trail: Give others' space and pace consideration. Steer clear of dominating the path or abrupt stops.

5. Reduce route Obstructions: To ensure the safety of other hikers, remove backpacks and other items off the route.

6. Reserve Quiet Spaces for Others: If you value solitude, think about going on hikes at off-peak hours or in less frequented locations to give others the opportunity to experience the same tranquilly.

More Advice on Proper Hiking Etiquette:

- Carefully evaluate the trail's difficulty, the weather, and your physical capabilities while planning your trek.

- Let someone know your intended return time and hiking itinerary.

- Bring gear and clothes suitable for the terrain and the weather.

- Bring along enough water and food to keep you nourished and alert.

Stay alert to your surroundings and any possible dangers, such drops that might be too steep or interactions with animals.

- Don't leave any signs of your visit, such as carvings or graffiti on rocks or trees.

- Show consideration for the customs and culture of the region you are trekking in.

- Show your support for neighborhood companies and communities by using their goods and services.

We can guarantee that everyone enjoys their outdoor experiences, that we have as little negative influence on the environment as possible, and that we leave the trails in the same beautiful condition that we found them by adhering to these hiking etiquette principles. Recall that safe hiking includes teamwork and care for other trail users. Together, let's protect our wilderness regions' pristine qualities for future generations.

5. ADDITIONAL INFORMATION

1. Best time to hike in Tenerife

With its varied hiking paths and stunning views, Tenerife, the enchanted island with volcanic scenery, lush woods, and sun-kissed beaches, entices travelers. Although the island is a year-round hiking destination, the ideal time to explore its trails will depend on your interests and the particular areas you choose to visit.

- **Spring: A Time of Awakening, March-May**

Tenerife is awash in color as springtime brings a riot of color to the landscapes thanks to the colorful display of blooming wildflowers. The paths are revitalized and the surrounding area is given a serene touch by the infrequent rains and nice temperatures.

- **Summer (June-August): Adventures in the Sun**

Summertime delivers bright, pleasant days that are ideal for seeing the island's upper altitudes. With its routes offering breathtaking views of Spain's highest peak, Mount Teide National Park, and its thick laurel woods, the Anaga Massif gives much-needed relief from the sun's heat.

- **Fall (September–November): A Colorful Symphony**

As the leaves begin to change color, autumn casts a golden tone over Tenerife's surroundings. It's the perfect time to take in the island's natural beauty in a more tranquil environment since the temperatures are still moderate and there are less people on the trails.

- **Winter: A Taste of Calm (December–February)**

When it comes to winter, Tenerife has a warmer climate than mainland Europe, with seldom any days below 15°C (59°F). This is the best time to see animals since the trails are less crowded and the island's distinctive flora and fauna are more active.

Attention to Particular Areas:

- **Mount Teide National Park**: During the winter, snow and ice conditions may occur at higher altitudes of Mount Teide; thus, it is advisable to monitor weather predictions and prepare for frigid temperatures.

- **Anaga Massif:** The luxuriant, sometimes slick vegetation of the Anaga Massif is well-known. On wet days, use caution and wear suitable footwear.

- **Coastal Trails:** Although coastal trails are usually open year-round, be prepared for occasional choppy waves and high gusts, particularly in the winter.

Guides for Selecting the Ideal Hiking Time:

- Take into account your own preferences: Summer is a wonderful option if you like warmer weather and don't mind crowds. Spring or fall may be a better option if you want less heat and less people.

- Make an itinerary: Find out which trails you want to walk and how accessible they are at various times of the year.

- Review weather forecasts: Keep an eye out for any possible weather, particularly at higher altitudes.

- Pack appropriately: Make sure you have the right clothes and equipment for the path conditions and the weather.

- Be adaptable: Be ready to modify your plans in the event that the weather changes.

Recall that Tenerife's hiking paths provide a year-round plethora of activities. You can make sure you have an amazing hiking experience on this charming island by taking your tastes into account, making a schedule, packing appropriately, and being adaptable.

Tenerife Navigation:

The biggest and most populated of the Canary Islands, Tenerife, has an alluring combination of sun-kissed beaches, lush woods, and volcanic scenery. Tenerife has something for everyone, whether you're looking for quiet getaway, cultural immersion, or outdoor experiences. Understanding the many available transit choices is key to appreciating the island's variety and beauty to the fullest. With the help of this in-depth guide, you'll be able to travel Tenerife with ease and have a wonderful trip.

Departing Tenerife

With two international airports, Tenerife is easily accessible from a wide range of locations worldwide. The primary hub of the island, Tenerife South Airport (TFS), sometimes referred to as Reina Sofía Airport, is where most foreign aircraft land. Los Rodeos Airport, popularly known as Tenerife North Airport (TFN), is mostly used for internal and inter-island flights.

Traveling to Your Location:

There are several ways to go from the airports to different areas of Tenerife. Take into account these choices for a convenient and enjoyable travel:

- **Taxis:** Direct transportation to your accommodation or destination is provided by taxis, which are easily found outside both airports. Because they are metered, taxi charges are clear.

- **Public Buses**: Major cities and well-liked tourist attractions are connected by Tenerife's vast public bus network, TITSA. Travel planning tools and comprehensive timetables are available on the Titsa website and mobile app.

- **Renting a vehicle**: You can explore Tenerife at your own speed with freedom and flexibility when you rent a vehicle. There are a lot of automobile rental companies on the island as well as at the airports.

- **Excursions and Tours**: With the assistance of knowledgeable local guides, organized excursions and tours provide a convenient method to see certain parts of Tenerife. These trips often involve activities, food, and transportation.

2. Getting to and around Tenerife:

Take into consideration these suggestions to guarantee a seamless and pleasurable travel experience in Tenerife:

- Arrange your schedule and travel requirements ahead of time.

- For convenience and cost savings, buy public transport tickets in advance.

- Learn the appropriate tipping amount and taxi etiquette.

- Give yourself enough time to travel, particularly during the busiest times of year.

- Be mindful of language difficulties and provide translation resources.

- Pay attention to the signage and traffic laws in your area.

Accept the relaxed pace of the island and enjoy the voyage.

Tenerife is waiting for you with its enthralling scenery, vibrant culture, and kind people. You'll be well-equipped to tour the island with ease if you comprehend the numerous transit alternatives and put these useful ideas to use. This will guarantee an amazing and fulfilling trip experience.

3. Accommodations in Tenerife

The biggest and most populated of the Canary Islands, Tenerife, provides a captivating combination of sun-kissed beaches, verdant woods, and volcanic vistas. Tenerife has something for everyone, whether you're looking for quiet getaway, cultural immersion, or outdoor experiences. Additionally, the island provides a broad range of lodging alternatives to suit every taste and price in order to meet the varied demands of its guests.

- **Hotels: A Variety of Amenities and Comforts**

For those who want a hassle-free and pleasant stay, hotels are a popular option. Tenerife is home to a wide selection of hotels, ranging in price from affordable lodgings to opulent resorts with a host of amenities including eating establishments, entertainment venues, and swimming pools.

Vacation Rentals and Aparthotels: Convenient Self-Catering

A more autonomous and self-catering alternative is offered by aparthotels and holiday rentals. With kitchens, living rooms, and bedrooms, these lodging options usually provide visitors the freedom to cook their own meals and take use of the conveniences of home while traveling.

- **Fincas and Villas: Privacy and Elegance**

For those looking for a little solitude and elegance, villas and fincas are a great option. These roomy lodgings, which are often surrounded by breathtaking surroundings, include private swimming pools, large patios, and fully functional kitchens, all of which contribute to a really remarkable and luxurious stay.

- **Countryside Hides: A Smell of Real Tenerife**

Consider booking a stay in a rustic lodge to see Tenerife at its most genuine. Nestled in quaint communities, these accommodations—often converted farmhouses or guesthouses—offer a window into the island's customs and way of life.

Hostels: Affordable and Social

For travelers on a tight budget, especially young explorers and backpackers, hostels provide a sociable and affordable alternative. Typically, hostels provide shared bathrooms, common spaces, and dormitory rooms to encourage a feeling of belonging and friendship among visitors.

Glamping and Camping: Getting Abundant with Nature

Glamping and camping provide an amazing experience for people looking to be close to nature. The island is home to a number of campgrounds that provide access to breathtaking natural settings and the chance to spend time in nature under the stars. An upgraded form of camping known as "glamping" has pre-erected tents or cabins with furnishings including mattresses, lights, and sometimes even private restrooms.

Attributes to Take Into Account While Selecting Housing:

Take into account the following elements while choosing a place to stay in Tenerife:

- Budget: There are a variety of lodging alternatives, from exquisite to affordable, so decide what you can afford to spend.

- Location: Choose lodging that is in a handy location for your activities after deciding the regions you want to see.

- Amenities: Think of the features that are essential to you, such as eating alternatives, spas, swimming pools, or self-catering accommodations.

- Travel Style: Whether it's a private villa, a communal hostel, or a rustic getaway, choose lodging that fits your preferred way of traveling.

- Travel Companions: When traveling with others, take into account their preferences and choose lodging that meets the requirements of all parties.

The variety of lodging choices available in Tenerife appeals to a broad spectrum of tourists, from discriminating luxury seekers to frugal backpackers. You may choose the ideal lodging to go along with your fantastic Tenerife trip by taking your preferences, spending limit, and style of travel into account.

4. Food and drink in Tenerife

The biggest and most populated of the Canary Islands, Tenerife, is well known for its rich culinary legacy in addition to its stunning scenery and lively culture. Travelers from all over the world are captivated by the island's food, which boasts a delicious blend of flavors and textures thanks to its volcanic origins, numerous cultural influences, and fresh local ingredients.

Mojo Sauces and Arrugadas: A Culinary Icon

A trip to Tenerife wouldn't be complete without sampling the famous wrinkled potatoes, or papas, and their mojo sauce accompaniments. A mainstay of Canarian cooking are these tiny, unpeeled potatoes, which are simmered in saltwater until their skins wrinkle. Traditionally, they are eaten with mojo picón, a fiery red sauce containing chili peppers, or mojo verde, a bright green sauce composed with garlic, cilantro, and olive oil.

Fresh Seafood: An Ocean Bounty

Tenerife's gastronomy is based mostly on fresh seafood, which is abundant due to the island's closeness to the Atlantic Ocean. The island's coastal cities and villages are a feast for the senses, offering everything from delicious whitebait and luscious grilled octopus to delicate (parrotfish) and robust seafood stews.

Gofio: A Mainstay with a Vast Past

A mainstay of Canarian cooking is gofio, a toasted grain flour prepared from a variety of grains, including wheat, barley and maize. Because of its adaptability, it may be used in a wide range of recipes, such as gofio , a straightforward porridge-like meal, and gofio amasado, a dough-like combination that is often served with cheese and roasted vegetables.

Wine from the Area: A Flavour of Volcanic Terroir

Tenerife has a long history of winemaking, and its volcanic terrain makes it an ideal place for viticulture. Strong reds from the south and delicate whites from the north are among the many great wines that are produced from the volcanic soils and distinct microclimates of the various areas.

Standard Desserts and Sweets: A Hint of Sweetness

Beyond its savory cuisine, Tenerife has a lovely assortment of traditional sweets and desserts to offer. Popular regional treats include quesillo, a baked egg custard resembling flan, and a rich and creamy almond custard. Savor the bananas that are characteristic to Tenerife, which are often served fried with honey or blended into pastries, for a taste of the island's tropical heritage.

Gastronomic Encounters and Tastes: Dive Into Flavour

If you want to really experience Tenerife's food culture, you might think about taking a cooking lesson or going on a guided food tour. These activities allow hands-on opportunity to learn traditional recipes, explore local ingredients, and appreciate the island's flavors under the supervision of skilled chefs and local experts.

As you go out on your Tenerife culinary adventure, let yourself be enthralled by the island's distinctive fusion of tastes, customs, and seasonal ingredients. Tenerife's cuisine offers a delicious culinary journey that will leave you with enduring memories, from the signature Papas Arrugadas and mojo sauces to the abundance of fresh fish and the distinctive flavor of local wines.

A Gastronomic Exploration of Tenerife: Revealing Tastes and Customs

The biggest and most populated of the Canary Islands, Tenerife, is well known for its rich culinary legacy in addition to its stunning scenery and lively culture. Travelers from all over the world are captivated by the island's food, which boasts a delicious blend of flavors and textures thanks to its volcanic origins, numerous cultural influences, and fresh local ingredients.

Mojo Sauces & Arrugadas: A Culinary Icon

A trip to Tenerife wouldn't be complete without sampling the famous wrinkled potatoes, or papas , and their mojo sauce accompaniments. A mainstay of Canarian cooking are these tiny, unpeeled potatoes, which are simmered in saltwater until their skins wrinkle. Traditionally, they are eaten with mojo picón, a fiery red sauce containing chili peppers, or mojo verde, a bright green sauce composed with garlic, cilantro, and olive oil.

Seafood that is fresh: A bounty from the sea

Tenerife's gastronomy is based mostly on fresh seafood, which is abundant due to the island's closeness to the Atlantic Ocean. The island's coastal cities and villages are a feast for the senses, offering everything from delicious whitebait and luscious grilled octopus to delicate (parrotfish) and robust seafood stews.

Gofio: A Mainstay with a Vast Past

A mainstay of Canarian cooking is gofio, a toasted grain flour prepared from a variety of grains, including wheat, barley and maize. Because of its adaptability, it may be used in a wide range of recipes, such as gofio , a straightforward porridge-like meal, and gofio amasado, a dough-like combination that is often served with cheese and roasted vegetables.

Wines from the Area: A Smell of Volcanic Terroir

Tenerife has a long history of winemaking, and its volcanic terrain makes it an ideal place for viticulture. Strong reds from the south and delicate whites from the north are among the many great wines that are produced from the volcanic soils and distinct microclimates of the various areas.

Customary Desserts & Sweets: A Hint of Sweetness

Beyond its savory cuisine, Tenerife has a lovely assortment of traditional sweets and desserts to offer. Popular regional treats include quesillo, a baked egg custard resembling flan, and a rich and creamy almond custard. Savor the bananas that are characteristic to Tenerife, which are often served fried with honey or blended into pastries, for a taste of the island's tropical heritage.

Tastes & Culinary Experiences: Lose Yourself in Flavour

If you want to really experience Tenerife's food culture, you might think about taking a cooking lesson or going on a guided food tour. Under the direction of seasoned chefs and local specialists, these experiences provide practical chances to learn traditional recipes, find local products, and enjoy the flavors of the island.

As you go out on your Tenerife culinary adventure, let yourself be enthralled by the island's distinctive fusion of tastes, customs, and seasonal ingredients. Tenerife's cuisine offers a delicious culinary journey that will leave you with enduring memories, from the signature Papas Arrugadas and mojo sauces to the abundance of fresh fish and the distinctive flavor of local wines.

CONCLUSION

Here are some more hiking advice for Tenerife:

- Make sure you dress appropriately for the weather and wear comfortable shoes.
- Bring snacks and plenty of water.
- Tell someone where you're going and when you should return.
- Keep an eye out for animals and be mindful of your surroundings.
- Be mindful of your surroundings and take away any traces of your existence.
- I hope your trekking experience in Tenerife is fantastic!

Tenerife hiking guide